Applied Rhythms

by Carl Palmer

Modern Drummer Publisher/CEO **David Frangioni**

Managing Director/SVP **David Hakim**

Editor **Rick Mattingly**
Design and Layout **David H. Creamer**
Digital Layout and Music Engraving **Terry Branam**
Transcriptions **William F. Miller**
Assistant Editor **Susan Hannum**

Published by:
Modern Drummer Publications, Inc.
1279 W Palmetto Park Rd
PO Box 276064
Boca Raton, FL 33427

**Subscribe to *Modern Drummer*, the world's best drumming magazine,
at: www.moderndrummer.com/subscribe**

**For fun and educational videos, subscribe to the
"Modern Drummer Official" YouTube channel.**

About the Author

Carl Palmer is one of the few drummers who have truly earned the title of "Legend." Born in Birmingham, England, on March 20, 1950, he began his drum studies at the age of 11 and studied with a number of prominent teachers. He then played in a number of local semipro groups in Birmingham, including the popular band The King Bees.

In 1965—at the age of 15—Carl moved to London to join Chris Farlowe & The Thunderbirds. Three years later, he became a member of The Crazy World of Arthur Brown (appearing on the hit record "Fire") and then led his own group, Atomic Rooster.

In 1970, he joined with keyboardist Keith Emerson and bassist/vocalist Greg Lake to form Emerson, Lake & Palmer. It was with this group that Carl achieved his reputation as a master of his instrument. The group combined classical influences with the power and volume of rock, resulting in music that was highly sophisticated but that reached a wide audience. Carl's virtuosic drum solos were always a highlight of ELP's live performances, and he was one of the first drummers to incorporate electronic drums into his setup.

Photo by Les Cole

When Emerson, Lake & Palmer broke up in the early '80s, Carl briefly led a band called PM. But soon afterward he joined with former Yes guitarist Steve Howe, former Yes keyboardist Geoff Downes, and former UK bassist/vocalist John Wetton to form the supergroup Asia. On the group's three albums (all of which were million sellers), Carl demonstrated a more basic, straight-ahead approach than he had used with ELP. But his blazing solos could still bring a crowd to its feet at live performances. In April 1987, Carl rejoined ELP.

Carl Palmer's recorded work has formed a legacy that ensures him a place in the history of drumming. But there is no reason to think that his best work is behind him. The legend will undoubtedly continue.

A NOTE FROM THE PUBLISHER

Carl Palmer's Applied Rhythms provides an awesome set of exercises and drumming 'tools" to improve your playing quickly and effectively. I've been inspired by Carl's playing since I was a child and first heard his virtuosic drumming with ELP.

In the 70s and 80's I dissected his technique the long way – by slowing down records and searching for any transcriptions that I could find. The deeper I went into his playing process, the more I learned as well as realizing that I had only scratched the surface!

Today we have Applied Rhythms and many of the techniques I wanted to learn from Carl are right here for us to study, practice and be inspired.

Thank you, Carl, for sharing the exercises, ideas and techniques that helped you learn and grow as a musician during your 50+ year legendary career. You're one of the greatest drummers to have ever played the instrument and an even better friend to know and always be inspired by!

David Frangioni
CEO/Publisher of Modern Drummer Publications, Inc.

Contents:

FOREWORD

My idea in writing the exercises in this book has been to create a selection of rhythms that can be used to develop the necessary technique that a modern drummer needs in a variety of situations. There is not an abundance of material here, but if you apply these rhythms in working situations, then you can get a lot out of this book.

Memorizing as many of these rhythms as possible after you have learned to play them will help you when you need to ad-lib around a particular rhythm. The best way to accomplish this is to play these exercises daily.

There is no given tempo for these exercises; each one should be played as relaxed as possible. Feel is the most important thing to remember; that is what should be achieved first.

I wish you the best of luck with this book and with your drumming.

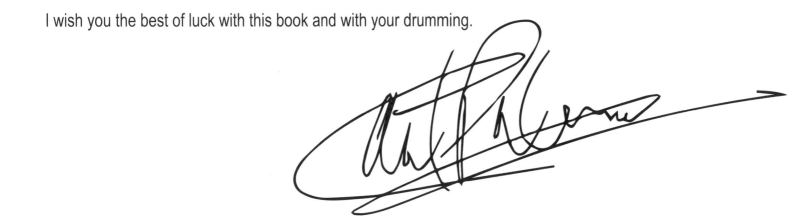

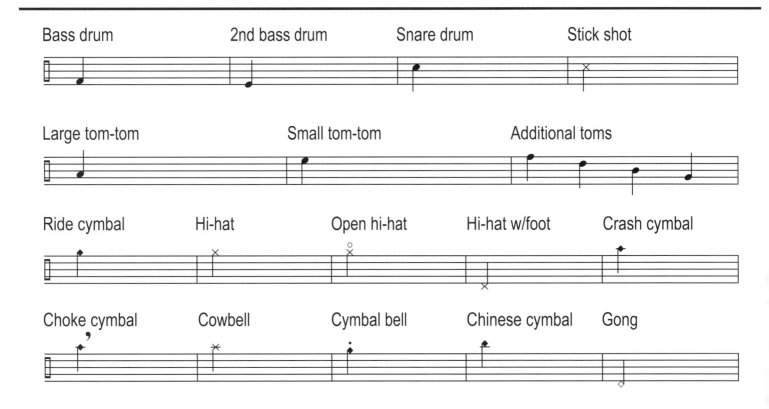

MODERN DRUMMER PUBLICATIONS

Chapter 1

This group of exercises is based around playing semiquavers (16th notes) between the hi-hat and snare drum. The object of this chapter is to make you familiar with leading with either the left or right hand, while playing various bass drum patterns. By the time you reach the end of this section, you will have played nearly every semiquaver in the bar on either the bass drum, or on the snare drum with either the left or right hand. So, after mastering these exercises, you will be quite familiar with reading this type of part.

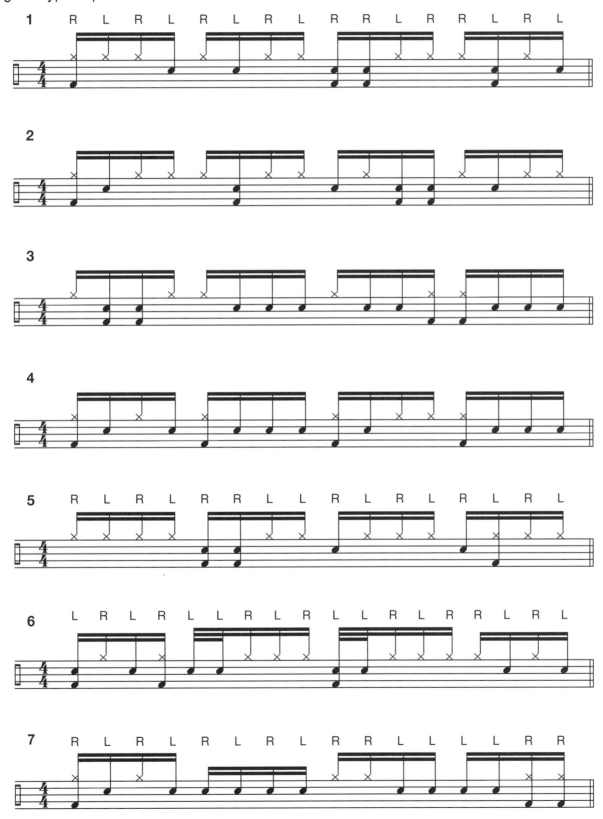

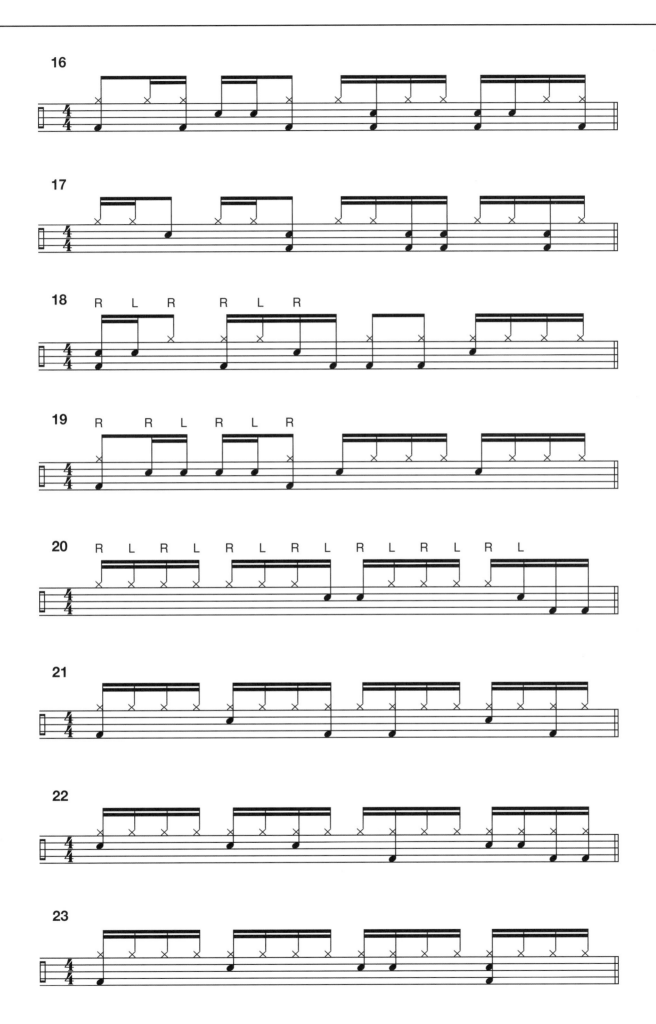

24

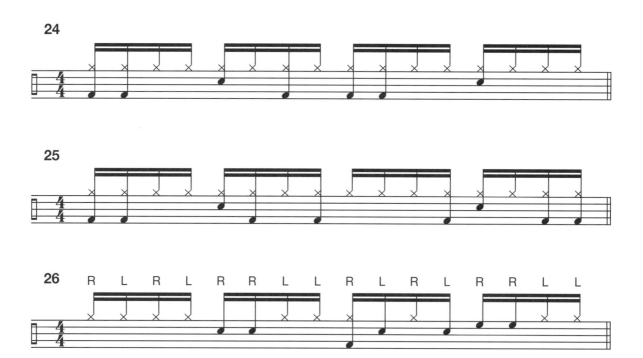

25

26

Chapter 2

This section deals with quavers (8th notes), which can be played on the hi-hat or ride cymbal, and with semiquaver (16th-note) triplets between the left hand and bass drum—something that became quite popular in the early '70s with various heavy rock bands. Basically, it started off as sort of a jazz pattern, but once it had been played on the bass drum instead of on the snare drum, it started to have a little more weight—hence the reason why heavy rock players would play this type of almost "fiddly" pattern. Nevertheless, it is quite complex and interesting to hear with the music.

These exercises deal with playing not only the last two beats of each semiquaver triplet, but also the first two. In addition, there are exercises that involve both triplets and straight semiquavers (i.e., exercise 9). You must practice these carefully so that the rhythms are precise, but it's worth it, because these patterns can be very effective when played correctly.

To see how I applied some of these concepts in an actual piece of music, see the transcription of "Jerusalem" elsewhere in this book. At letter C in that chart, I played triplets between the bass drum and the snare drum/hi-hat.

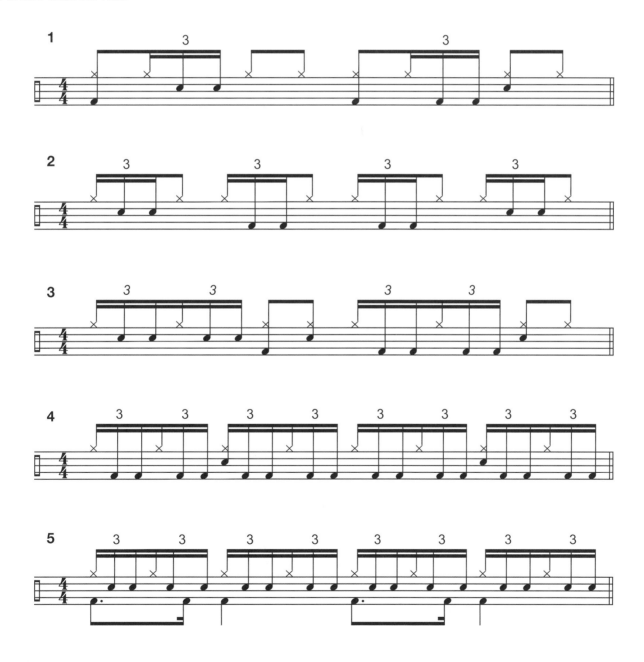

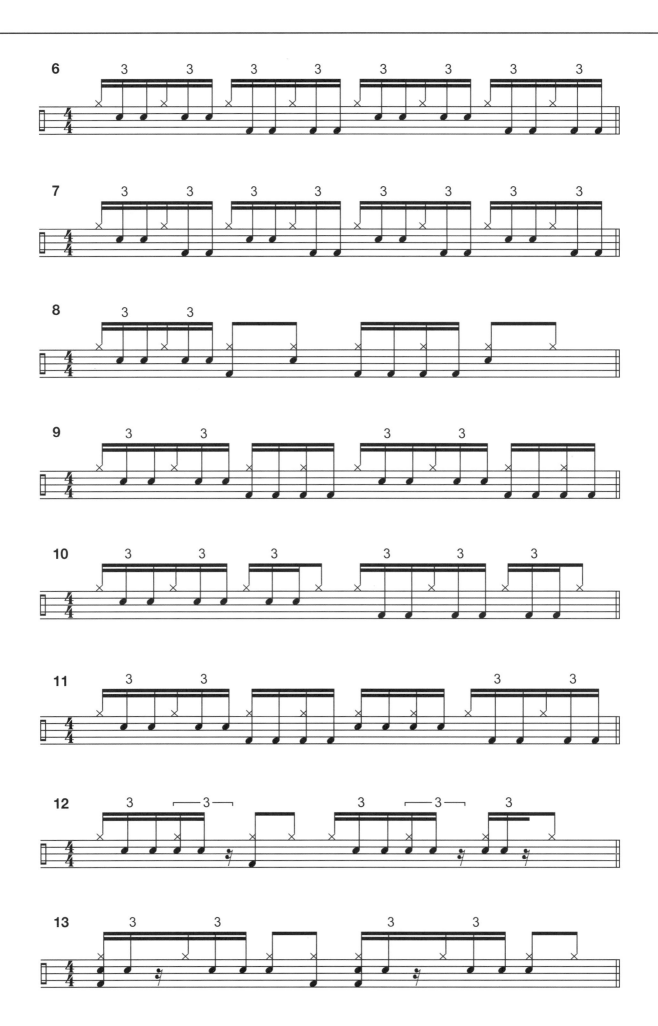

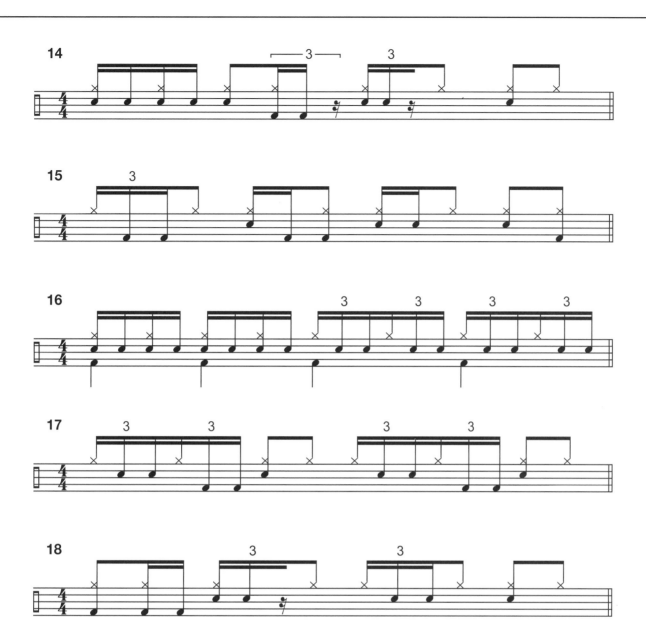

Chapter 3

These exercises deal with several things. The idea here is to make you familiar with playing not only quavers (8th notes) and semiquavers (16th notes), but odd quavers with the left hand on the hi-hat, which has become quite popular over the years. I've also written the odd tom-tom or cowbell note, and I find that this is something that is quite interesting. In exercise 3, play all of the ride cymbal quavers with the right hand while playing the closed hi-hat (notated on the fourth space in this example) and snare drum with the left hand. In exercise 6, you will play all of the offbeat quavers in the bar with the right hand on the cymbal (which is sometimes known as the "pea soup pattern"), while your left hand plays both semiquaver triplets and straight semiquavers. Exercise 9 is in 6/4 time, and it incorporates a fill along with a drum pattern. These exercises are all a little different, and they bring the material from Chapters 1 and 2 into more of a musical context.

Chapter 4

When you look at these exercises, the first thing you might think is that it looks like a step backwards; it doesn't look as if we've advanced from Chapter 3. But the idea of the exercises in this chapter is to make you familiar with playing not only quavers (8th notes) and semiquavers (16th notes), but also straight crotchets (quarter notes), which obviously would change the sound of the exercises completely. That's the object here. Once you've mastered playing straight quavers on the hi-hat or the ride cymbal, change the quavers to crotchets, which gives a different feel altogether—especially when you are playing semiquavers on the bass drum or in the left hand while playing crotchets with the right hand. So these exercises really are a double set of exercises to be played both with quavers on the cymbal (or hi-hat) and with crotchets.

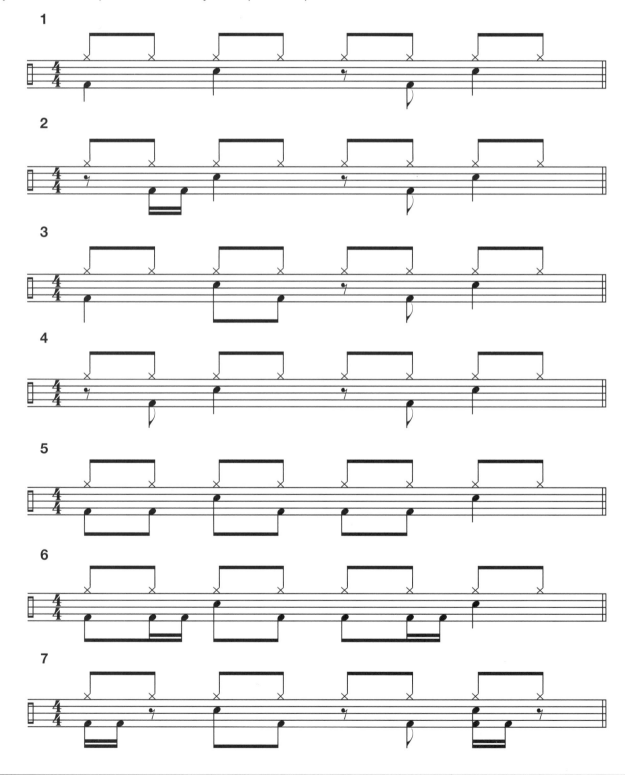

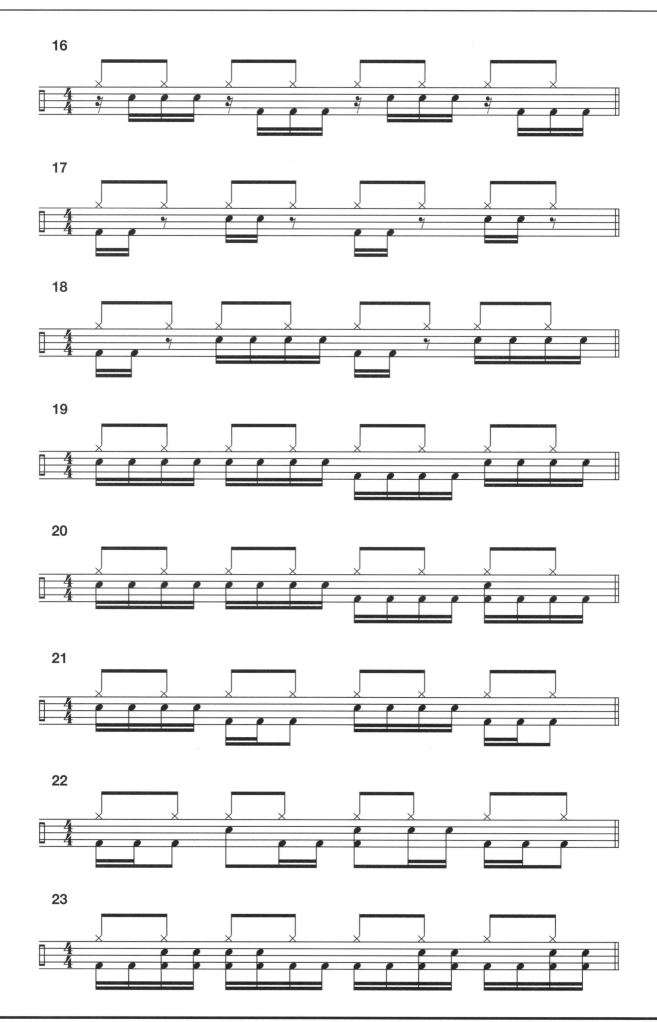

Chapter 5

These exercises produce an almost Latin/rock type of sound. The right-hand pattern should be played on the bell of the ride cymbal. The cymbal rhythm is a little bit hard to lock into at first, because it's not a basic, straight rhythm. It has quaver (8th) and semiquaver (16th) notes in it; as I said, it's a little bit Latin sounding. But once you have shifted onto "automatic pilot" and you have this rhythm in your right hand, the left-hand parts are really the most interesting. That's what this section is all about: getting the left hand working a little more against the right, with the bass drum keeping a very steady pulse.

I've also involved "stick shots"; that's when one places the stick across the rim and gets a kind of "rimshot" sound. I've found that quite effective with this bell rhythm in the right hand. In exercise 9, while playing four-to-the-bar on the bass drum and the Latin cymbal rhythm with the right hand, you've got a combination of stick shots and regular snare drum beats with the left hand. So here you have to get very familiar with changing the position of your left hand on the drum in order to obtain the two sounds, while reading the rhythms. I've involved this technique in three of the exercises, and it proves to be quite a nice flavor .

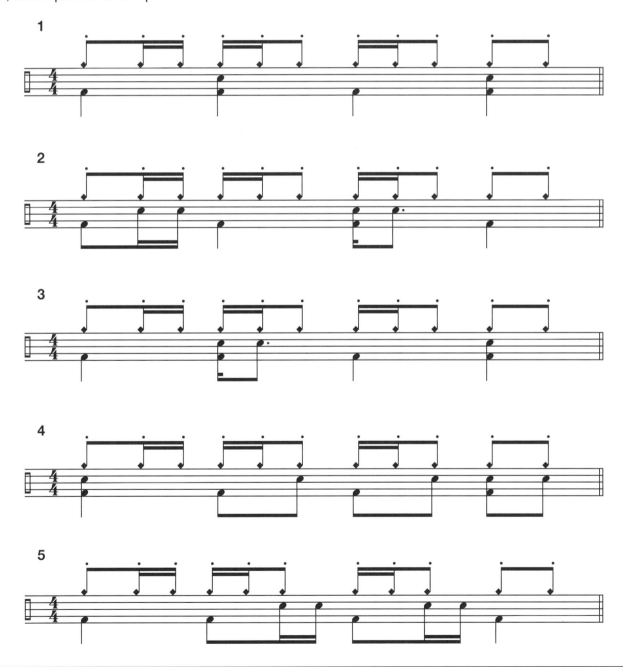

Chapter 6

This section continues with the Latin/rock approach to playing time on the bell of the cymbal, but this time there are semiquavers (16th notes), quavers (8th notes), and crotchets (quarter notes) with the left hand and bass drum. This is quite a large step forward from the previous chapter. There are some very nice exercises in this section; it happens to be one of my favorites. These are quite tricky to play, but very interesting and most enjoyable for me.

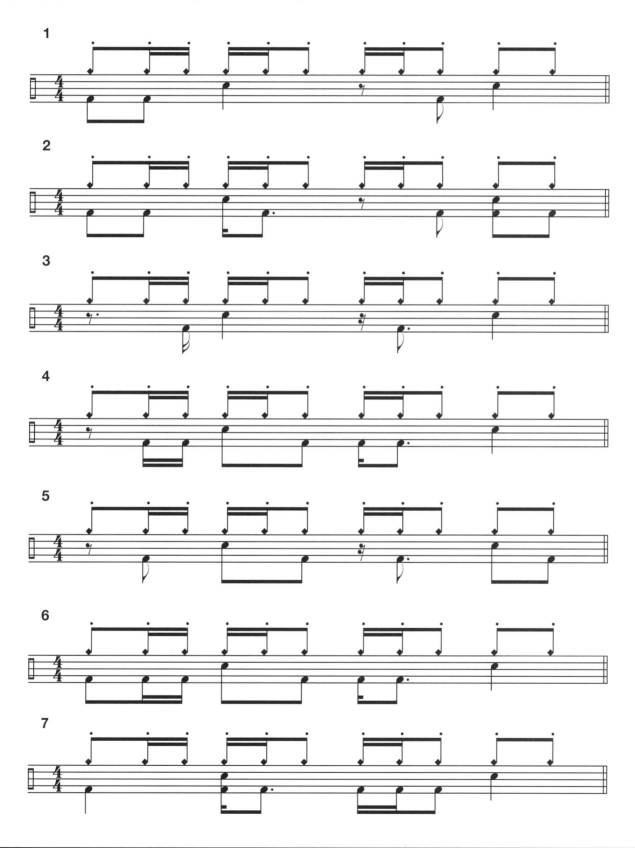

8

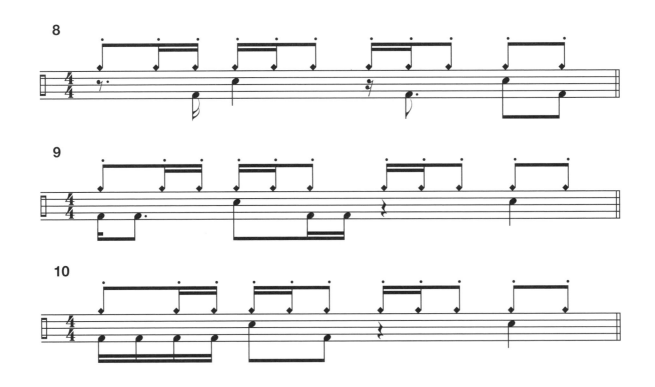

9

10

Chapter 7

These exercises use semiquavers (16th notes) again, but this time they are all played with the right hand on the hi-hat or ride cymbal. The bass drum and snare drum patterns deal with quavers (8th notes), crotchets (quarter notes), and semiquavers. The idea of these exercises is to enable you to play complex bass drum/snare drum rhythms against a 16th-note feel at slower tempos. Again, there are no tempo markings on these exercises, because it's the individual feel that matters. If you can obtain a good feel at a slower tempo, then it's better to play it slow than fast. The exercises in Chapter 7 are all meant to be played at slower tempos, so that you can concentrate on obtaining a very steady 16th-note feel with one hand.

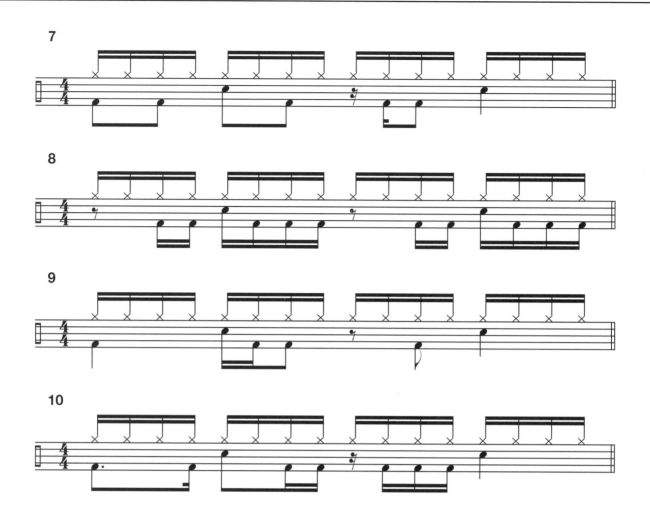

Chapter 8

This chapter contains a series of fills that can be learned separately from the actual drum patterns. The idea here is to flam various quavers (8th notes) in the bar, and to voice the quavers around the drumset in different ways—between snare drum and small tom-tom, between floor tom-tom and snare drum, etc. The ten exercises in this chapter consist of one-bar drum fills that can, obviously, be repeated twice. The first time, you could read them as written; the second time, you could voice them differently. So that gives you the option to choose your own voicings but still keep the rhythmical sound that I've written down. Another good way to practice these fills is to combine them with the exercises in the previous chapters. Basically they're all quavers here—very, very simple to play, but very effective if executed with the right amount of taste.

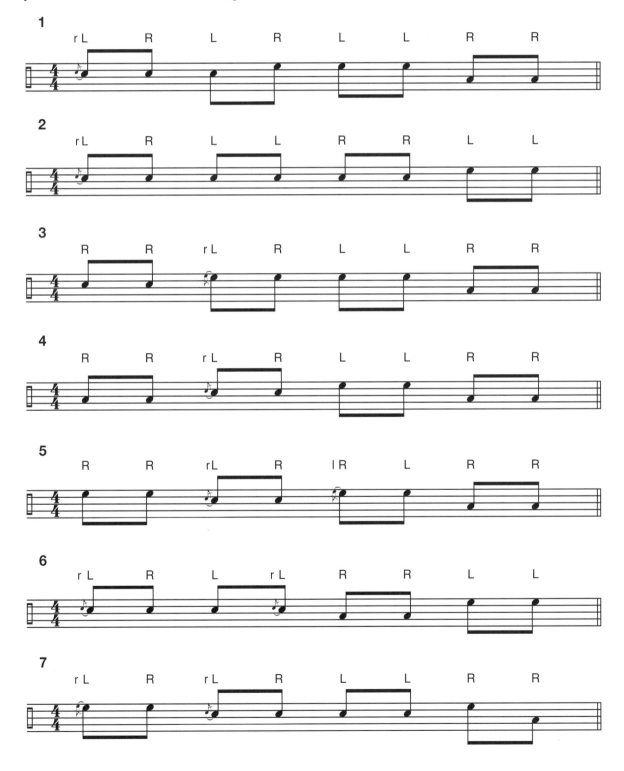

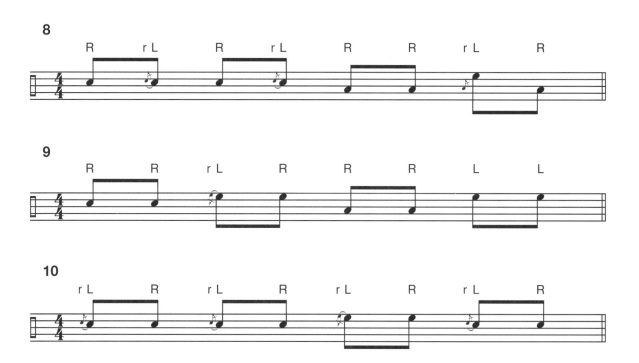

Chapter 9

This section is very similar to Chapter 8, except that this time I've decided to deal with semiquavers (16th notes). The semiquavers are over the space of two straight crotchets (quarter notes); in other words, it's a drum fill that takes up half a bar. I've used eight semiquavers and flammed them in various places. These drum fills work well for tempos that are a little bit faster, but you should first find a tempo that is appropriate to your individual technique. These fills are written all on the snare drum, and there's a funky, almost military sound that you obtain by playing them in this fashion. The last section of the song "Heat Of The Moment" is similar to these exercises. For other examples of the ways in which I use flams in my playing, see the transcriptions of "Jerusalem" and "Letters From The Front."

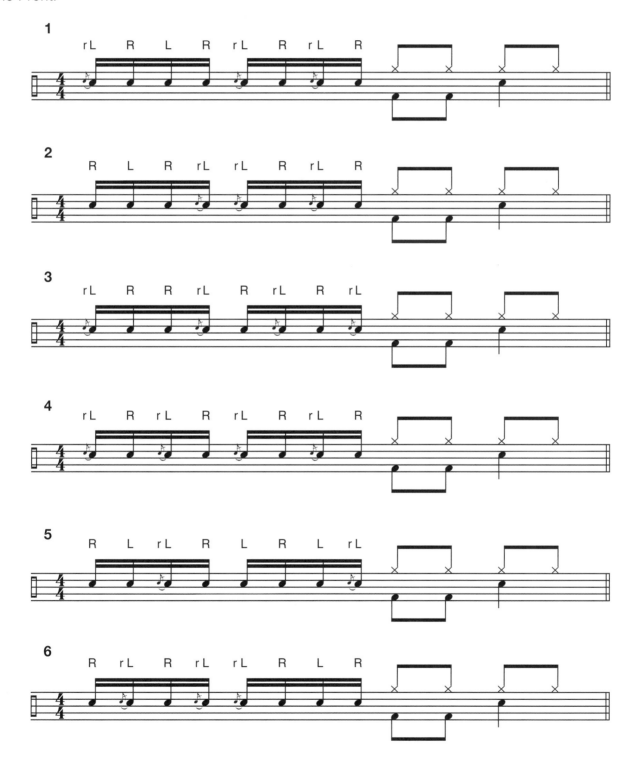

Chapter 10

This chapter, in actual fact, is a combination of the exercises from the first seven chapters. The only new thing that's being introduced here is demisemiquavers (32nd notes) between the bell of a cymbal and the snare drum, which gives a fast, sort of "rumbling" effect. There are ten exercises in all, and basically, if you have gone through the previous chapters in the book, you should be able to read this section reasonably quickly. These patterns are all very individual sounding, although they may not be the best of exercises for actually playing with a band. I do call the book *Applied Rhythms*, and these <u>can</u> be applied, but the thing is that they are extremely complex, so they could only be applied if something were actually worked out and arranged within a group. They're not the kind of patterns that you could simply throw in and obtain the most from. But if they were worked into the arrangement, then obviously these would be most beneficial.

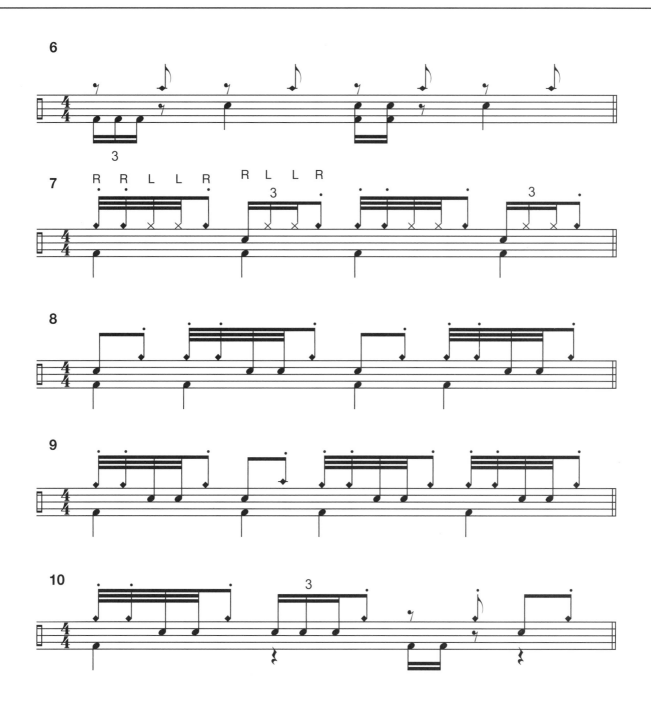

DON'T CRY

Asia: *Alpha* (Geffen GHS 4008)
Recorded 1983

For anyone with a limited reading ability, I would suggest that "Don't Cry" would be the easiest to start off with. It's very, very basic—possibly the kind of drum part that most drummers wish they didn't have put in front of them because it's so, so simple. But when you create a drum part around a song that's aimed at being a single, you end up having to be quite basic in your approach. So this is a very basic drum part but very good for people who want to try their hand at reading. The fills that are there—a couple of flams and semiquavers—are things that we have already practiced in the book, so there's absolutely nothing here that you haven't seen before. It's just all put together. So I would say that "Don't Cry" is definitely a great starter for anyone wanting to go through the different pieces of drum music in this book .

fade out

HARD ON ME

Asia: *Astra* (Geffen GHS 24072)
Recorded 1985

"Hard On Me" is an uptempo rock track from the *Astra* album. There are a couple of interesting timbale fills here, which is the first time I used them on this particular album. There's a nice thing at the very end where there are three crotchet triplets followed by a crotchet—a very jumpy, almost machine-like fill. This track was basically written, recorded, and mixed within four to five days. It happens to be one that I co-wrote, so I'm quite pleased with it.

(Simmons)

GO

Asia: *Astra* (Geffen GHS 24072)
Recorded 1985

"Go" is basically a very straightforward rock track. This was Asia's equivalent to Van Halen's "Jump." There are some groups of sixes, which I usually don't play, just before letter D. The rest of the piece is pretty standard. It's a normal sort of bass drum pattern. There are two bass drums at the end on a fill, which is one of the few times I've actually used two bass drums in a fill. I usually play the two bass drums in ensemble passages, but this time was used just for one fill.

fade out

Photo by Les Cole

HEAT OF THE MOMENT

Asia: *Asia* (Geffen GHS 2008)

Recorded 1981

"Heat Of The Moment" was Asia's very first number-one single. The drum part is very simple. There are a couple of odd bars here and there—nothing really to worry anybody. There's a nice middle-8 section where there are semiquavers on the hi-hat and accents on the bass drum. There's not much to panic about on this one. During the last part of the song, which is a guitar solo, all of the actual rhythm is played on the snare drum—almost a military feel. It's a slow tempo, so I don't think it will be much of a problem for people who are not so great at reading. It's a little more complex than "Don't Cry" but still fairly easy. The back half of "Heat Of The Moment" is probably the area that should be looked at first because that is the hardest part. Apart from that, it's a good all-around drum part. There's a cowbell section, a section of straight fours on the hi-hat, and a good snare drum part. So it gets you around the drumset playing different colors and sounds, and the song has a really nice melody to play along with. It's not a piece that you get bored with because the tune is so good.

SOLE SURVIVOR

Asia: *Asia* (Geffen GHS 2008)
Recorded 1981

"Sole Survivor" was one of the first pieces of music that Asia recorded. The drum part is quite interesting because it has various sections where bars of 4/4 go into bars of 3/4 and 2/4. Normally, the music with Asia was quite consistent—always in 4/4 meter—but on this particular piece there are some interesting time changes. It's quite interesting to play and will probably take a little more time to learn than the others. Also, as you can see on the part, there are two bass drums at the end, which is something that has become quite popular over the years. When playing this double-bass part, I lead with my right foot. I find it quite enjoyable to play this particular piece. I think it speaks for itself once you see the actual music—a very, very good piece of music in general.

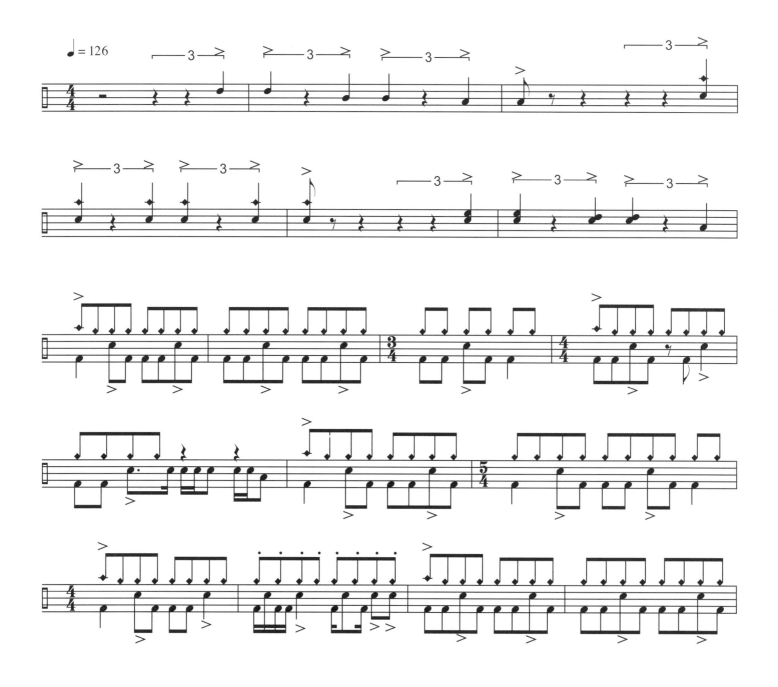

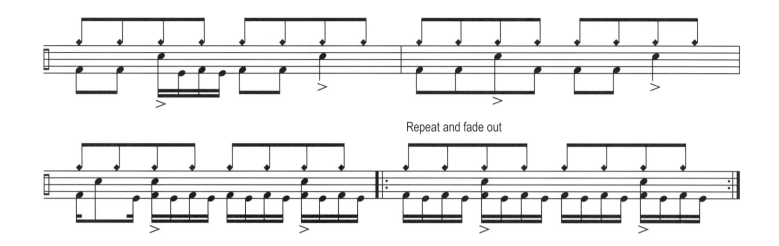

Repeat and fade out

Photo by Ebet Roberts

TIME AGAIN

Asia: *Asia* (Geffen GHS 2008)
Recorded 1981

"Time Again" is the only drum part here that deals with a shuffle rhythm. Along with "Letters From The Front," "Time Again" is probably one of the more interesting parts and is for the more advanced players. I say that because there are some different time signatures. There are bars of 4/4, 12/8, 3/4, and 6/8; the very end of it might be a little tricky for some people at first. There are some double bass drum fills and some flam fills, which we've seen in the exercises in the book.

When I approached this piece of music, I thought, "If this were an orchestra rather than a group, how would the drum part develop?" That's exactly what I've done. For example, nine bars after letter A, there's a typical sort of big band accent that I play on the cymbals, snare drum, and bass drum in unison, which is something you'd usually find in the Woody Herman orchestra or the Buddy Rich band. Though "Time Again" was recorded by a rock group, it looks to me—and I've seen quite a few of them—like a big band drum part. I suggest that the golden rule for learning all of these parts should be to play them first without the record, so that you play them accurately and understand completely what's going on.

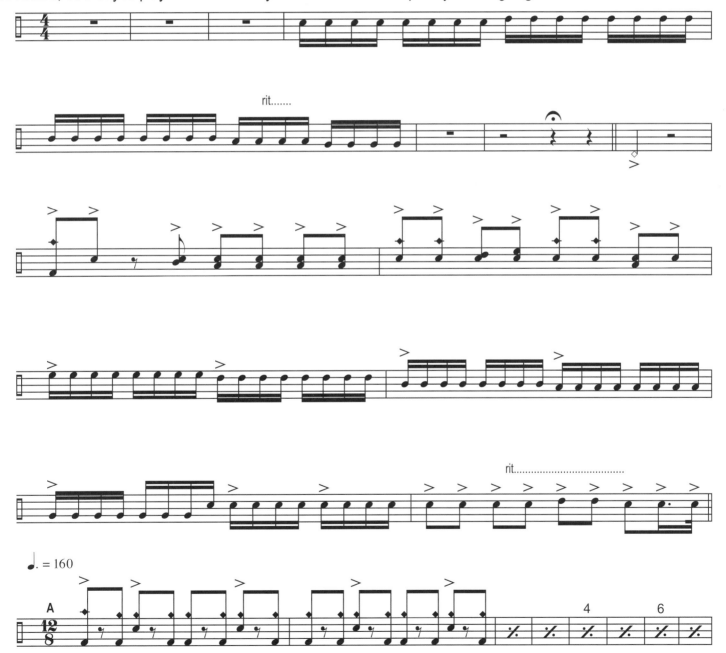

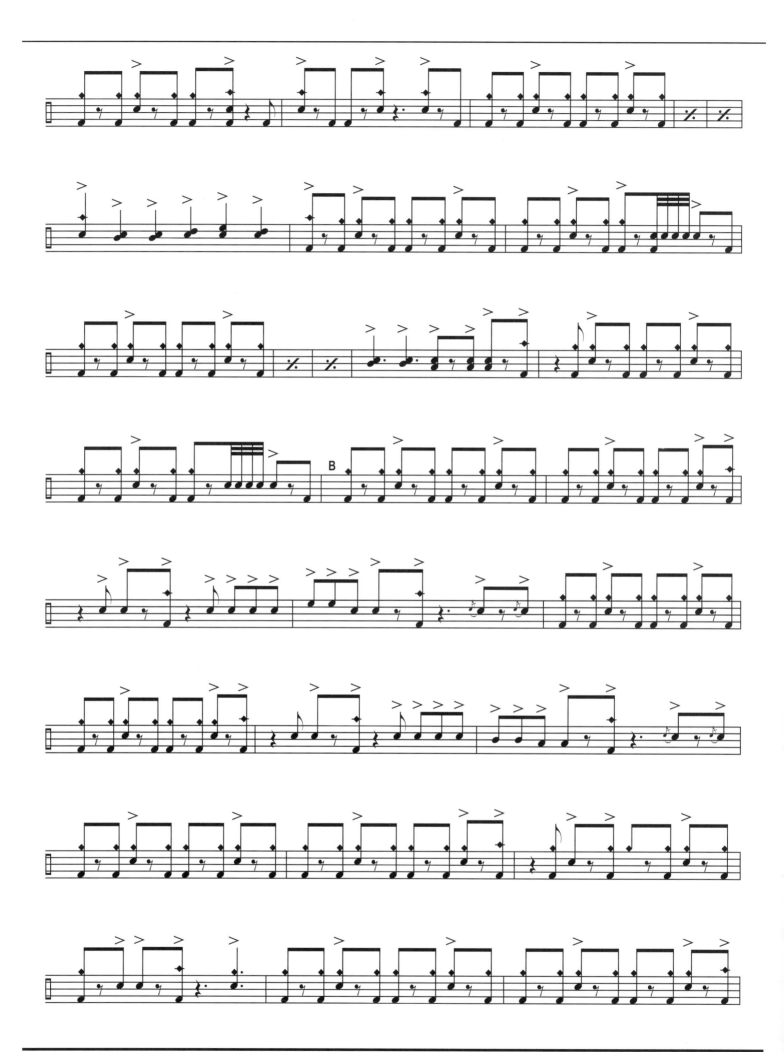

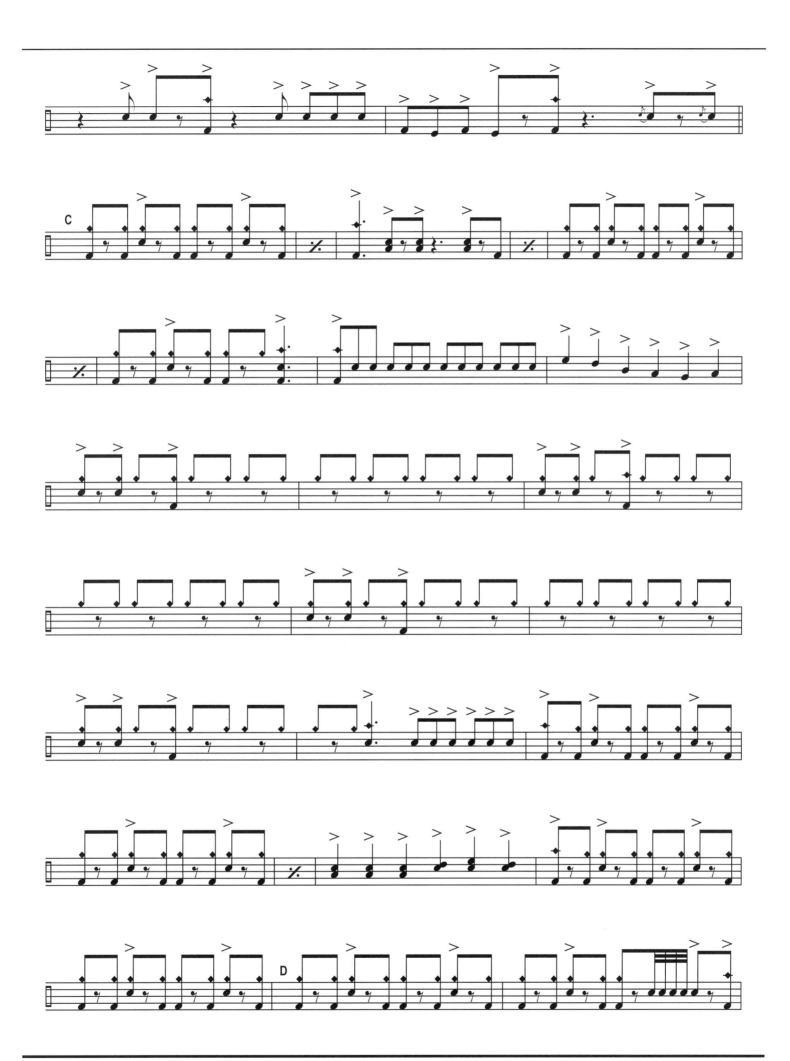

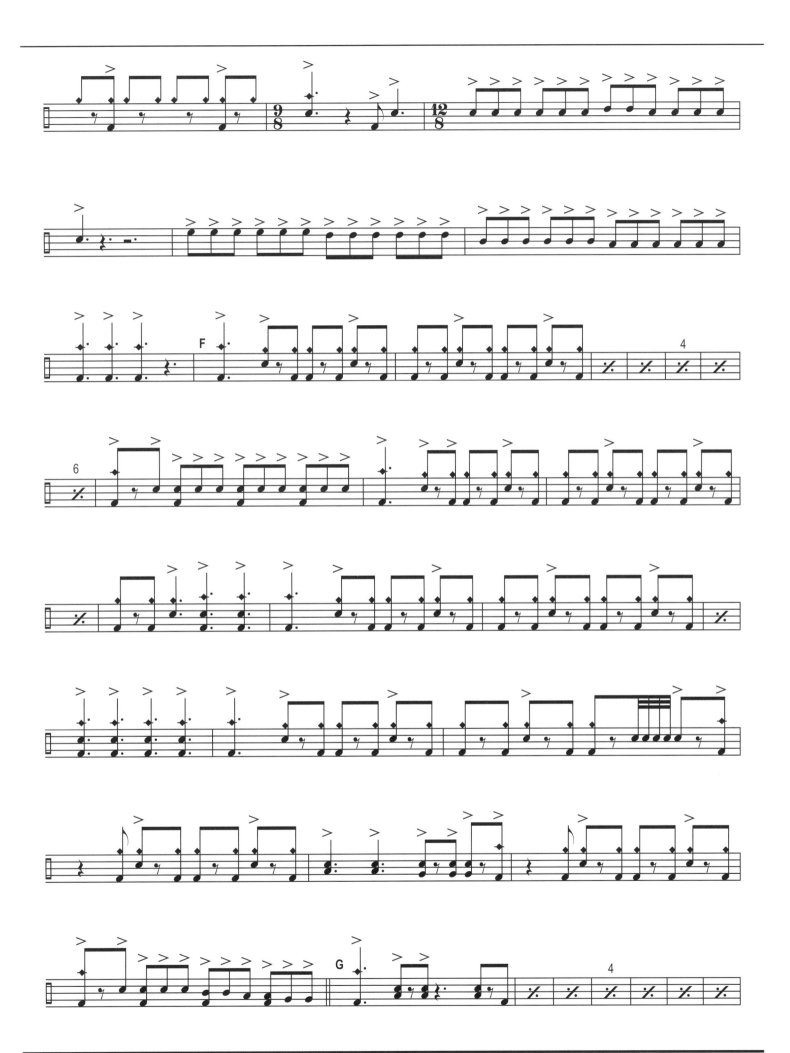

HOEDOWN

Emerson, Lake, & Palmer: *Trilogy* (Atlantic SD 19123)
Recorded 1972
(This tune also appears on the live album *Welcome back, my friends, to the show that never ends.....*
Manticore MC-3-200, recorded 1974)

This is one of my favorite instrumentals—probably one of the all-time great pieces of music I played
with Emerson, Lake, & Palmer. Without a shadow of a doubt, it's one of my favorites and the only piece
of music I've ever played by Aaron Copeland. I'm sure that I'll play this piece again in the future.

This part is basically lifted from the orchestral arrangement. I've adapted the percussion parts that the
orchestra would have played as closely as I could put them on the drums. Four bars after letter C is a
very typical Aaron Copeland brass sort of phrase. I play that one with the band (or with the orchestra,
depending on which record you're listening to). This is a very good part for the student to learn,
because it is a little more diverse. It's not just four on the floor with a bass drum. There are some quite
interesting accents that have to be played. They're unexpected, and they come in at strange times. But
basically, it's 4/4 throughout, so there shouldn't be any problem with playing this one.

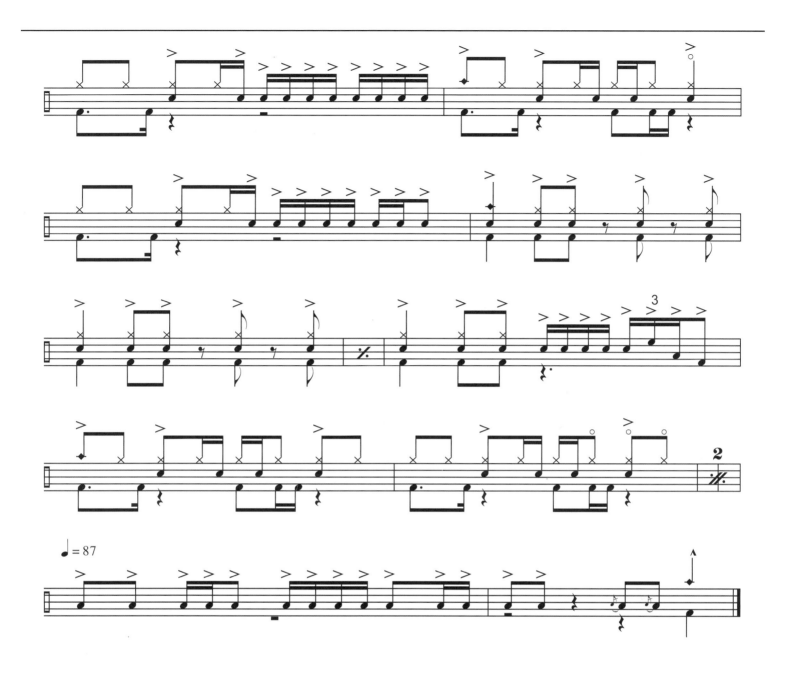

JERUSALEM

Emerson, Lake, & Palmer: *Brain Salad Surgery* (Atlantic SD 19124)
Recorded 1973

"Jerusalem" was banned in England on the radio. Although we tried to get a very orchestral feel, as with all the pieces of music that we played with Emerson, Lake, & Palmer, it was still labeled as a piece of pop music. For that alone, the BBC would not accept "Jerusalem" as a serious piece of music. Even though "Jerusalem" itself is a very serious piece of church music, the BBC thought we were degrading it.

Nevertheless, the drum part to this is interesting. There are some groups of sixes and rolls going in a clockwise direction around the drumset. There's a lot of rolling in this. This is an exercise in playing a single-stroke roll across the tom-toms while still trying to keep time. Though the timpani and chimes parts have been excluded and only the basic drum part has been written, chimes, timpani, and drums can be played all by the same person, as I did on the recording of this particular song. This is a great piece of music, a good drum part, and I hope you have lots of fun with it.

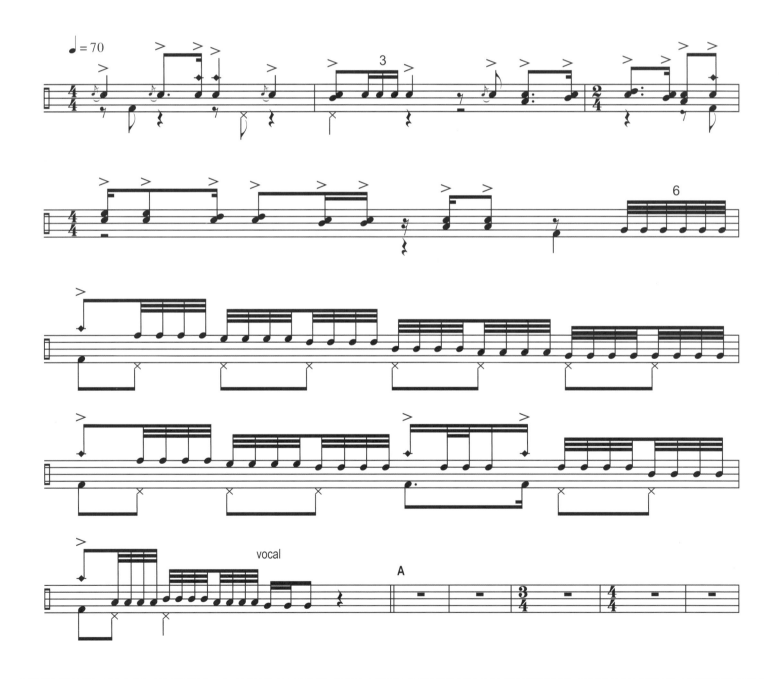

MODERN DRUMMER PUBLICATIONS

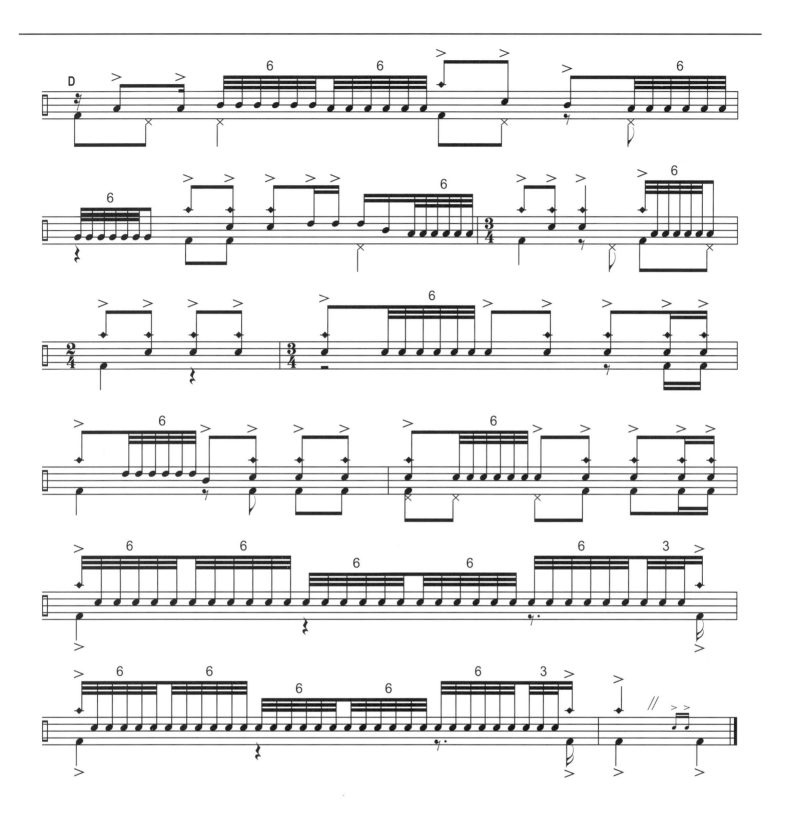

LETTERS FROM THE FRONT

Emerson, Lake, & Palmer: *Love Beach* (Atlantic SD 19211)
Recorded 1978

"Letters From The Front" was one of the very last pieces of music recorded by Emerson, Lake, & Palmer. This is one of my favorite drum parts—quite intricate. One really has to concentrate on the bass drum/snare drum patterns. There are quite a lot of fills and things that are a little off-the-wall, and there are some nice changes in tempo and meter. I think that the music has some really good reading exercises in it that would definitely enable players to read parts in the future a lot easier. It's quite complex in places, and it's probably one of the best drum parts in the book.

I would suggest that you first go through it without the record and really get the hang of it because, by playing it only with the record, you might be inclined to miss a few of the little intricacies. The odd 5/4 bar or the odd 2/4 bar does need a certain amount of attention. The last part of the song from section D is quite interesting because it has some bars that are played in unison between bass and drums. Those are quite effective on record, and obviously quite good from a reading point of view because this means that you have to be counting strict time. In other words, you're not actually playing, and then you must come back in at the proper time.

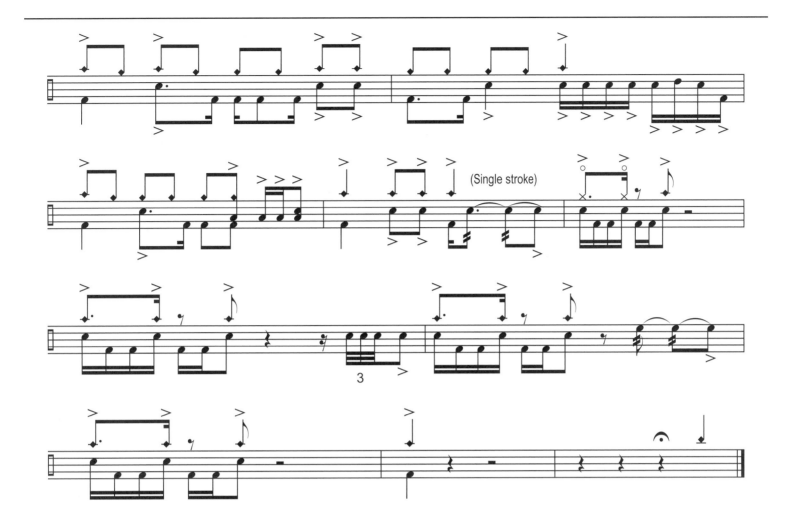

(Single stroke)

3

BRAIN SALAD SURGERY

Emerson, Lake, & Palmer: *Works; Vol 2* (Atlantic SD 19124)
Recorded 1977

This particular piece of music deals with some good time signatures—3/4, 4/4, 7/8, and 5/8. Actually, if you play the record and look at the music here, you can hear that it's a lot easier to play than it looks. It looks complicated, but it's quite a melodic piece of music, and the drums basically are doubling up many of the melodic figures—playing in unison with the piano, the keyboards, or whatever's happening at the time.

This is for more advanced players who really want to get their teeth into playing different time signatures. It is probably one of the most musical pieces, from the drumming point of view, in the book—definitely more complex than most. There's nothing that goes through this piece that's constant. It's changing literally all the time.

Before attempting the beginning of this piece, you might try starting at letter B. This is where the 3/4 time feel begins and the vocal part enters. Learning this section first will ease you into the piece. The 3/4 time signature is not used in rock that often, and the pattern at letter B has a nice feel to it.